Microsoft Excel 2013 Expert

Michelle N. Halsey

Silver City Publications & Training, L.L.C.
P.O. Box 1914
Nampa, ID 83653
https://www.silvercitypublications.com/shop/

ISBN-10: 1-64004-043-9
ISBN-13: 978-1-64004-043-4

Contents

Chapter 1 – Working with Permissions and Options

This chapter introduces you to the Information tab on the Backstage View. You will learn about marking a workbook as final, which makes the workbook read-only. You will also learn about permissions – both encrypting the workbook with a password and restricting permissions. This chapter explains how to protect both the current sheet and an entire workbook's structure. You will also learn how to add a digital signature, which is helpful if your workbook contains macros that you want to share with others. Then we will move on to exploring the Excel options dialog box, where you can set advanced options and properties. We will look at managing versions, which can help you recover unsaved work if you have Autosave turned on. Finally, we will look at saving your workbook as a template to simplify new workbook creation.

Marking a Workbook as Final

To mark a workbook as final, use the following procedure.

Step 1: Select the **File** tab from the Ribbon to open the Backstage View.

Step 2: Select **Protect Workbook**.

Step 3: Select **Mark as Final**.

Step 4: Excel displays a warning message. Select **OK** to continue.

Step 5: Excel displays an information message. Select **OK** to continue.

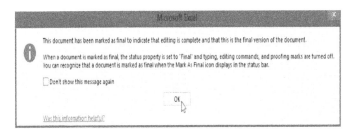

Notice the yellow bar at the top of the workbook to indicate that the workbook has been marked as final.

Notice that on the Info tab on the Backstage View, the Permissions area has changed.

Encrypting with a Password

To encrypt a workbook with a password, use the following procedure.

Step 1: Select the **File** tab from the Ribbon to open the Backstage View.

Step 2: Select **Protect Workbook**

Step 3: Select **Encrypt with Password**.

Step 4: In the *Encrypt Document* dialog box, enter the password that you want to use.

Step 5: In the *Confirm Password* dialog box, re-enter the password that you want to use to confirm it.

Note that if you want to remove the password protection, you will repeat the process. However, leave the password field blank.

Protecting the Current Sheet or the Workbook Structure

To protect a current sheet of a workbook, use the following procedure.

Step 1: Select the **File** tab from the Ribbon to open the Backstage View.

Step 2: Select **Protect Workbook**.

Step 3: Select **Protect Current Sheet**.

Step 4: Excel displays the *Protect Sheet* dialog box.

Step 5: You can enter a password if desired to unprotect the sheet.

Step 6: Check the boxes for the actions that you want to allow other users to perform on the sheet.

Step 7: Select **OK**.

To protect a workbook structure, use the following procedure.

Step 1: Select the **File** tab from the Ribbon to open the Backstage View.

Step 2: Select **Protect Workbook**.

Step 3: Select **Protect Workbook Structure**.

Step 4: Excel displays the *Protect Structure and Windows* dialog box.

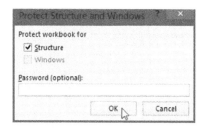

Step 5: Check the boxes for the options you want to protect.

Step 6: You can enter a password if desired to unprotect the workbook.

Step 7: Select **OK**.

Adding a Digital Signature

To add a digital signature to a workbook, use the following procedure.

Step 1: Select the **File** tab from the Ribbon to open the Backstage View.

Step 2: Select **Protect Workbook**.

Step 3: Select **Add a Digital Signature**.

Step 4: Excel may display an informational message. Select **OK**.

Step 5: In the **Sign** dialog box, select the **Commitment Type** from the drop down list.

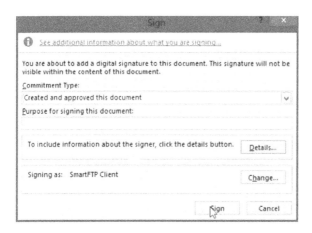

Step 6: Enter a **Purpose** for signing the document.

Step 7: If you would like to include additional information about the signer, select **Details**.

Step 8: In the *Additional Signing Information* dialog box, enter the signature information and select **OK**.

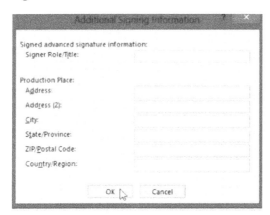

Step 9: Your **Signature Certificate** should appear in the **Signing as** area. If not, select **Change** and choose a new one from the *Windows Security* dialog box.

Step 10: Select **Sign**.

Step 11: The *Signature Confirmation* dialog box displays. Select **OK**.

Setting Excel Options

To review the options for customizing Excel, use the following procedure.

Step 1: Select the **File** tab from the Ribbon to open the Backstage view.

Step 2: Select the **Options** tab on the left.

Step 3: Here is the **General** tab in the Excel Options dialog box. The General tab allows you to change the user interface options. You can enter your name or initials to personalize your copy of Excel.

Here is the **Formulas** tab in the Excel Options dialog box. The Formulas tab controls your Calculation options, how you work with formulas, your error checking options, and the error checking rules.

Here is the **Proofing** tab in the Excel Options dialog box. The Proofing tab allows you to control how Autocorrect works for spelling.

Here is the **Save** tab in the Excel Options dialog box. The Save tab allows you to control how workbooks are saved.

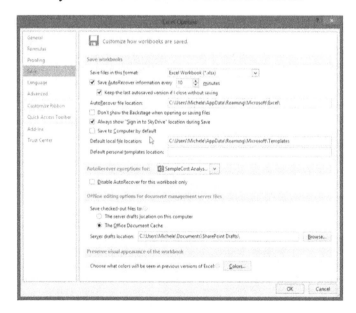

Here is the **Language** tab in the Excel Options dialog box. The Language tab controls your editing language and your display and help language.

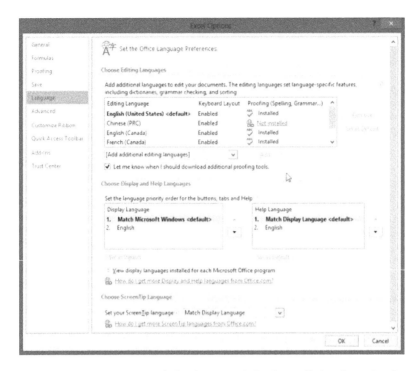

Here is the **Advanced** tab in the Excel Options dialog box. In the Advanced tab, you can change a number of editing options, including the default paste option and options when calculating the workbook.

Managing Versions

To use the Manage Versions feature, use the following procedure.

Step 1: Select the **File** tab from the Ribbon to open the Backstage view.

Step 2: Select **Info**, if it is not already selected.

Step 3: The Versions area includes the most recent versions of the workbook. You can select one to return to it.

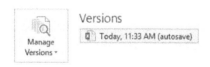

Step 4: Or, select **Manage Versions**.

Step 5: Select **Recover Unsaved Workbooks**.

Step 6: The *Open* dialog box displays a list of your unsaved files. Highlight the file and select **Open**.

Step 7: Make sure you save the file.

Saving a Workbook as an Excel Template

To set the default template location, use the following procedure.

Step 1: Select the **File** tab from the Ribbon to open the Backstage view.

Step 2: Select the **Options** tab on the left.

Step 3: Select the **Save** tab.

Step 4: In the **Default personal templates location** field, enter the path to the templates folder you have created.

To save the current workbook as a template, use the following procedure.

Step 1: Select the **File** tab from the Ribbon to open the Backstage View.

Step 2: Select **Save As.**

Step 3: In the *Save As* dialog box, select **Excel Template (*xltx)** from the **Save as Type** drop down list.

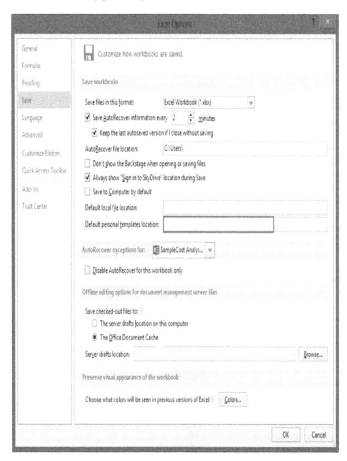

Notice that when you make that selection, the navigation changes to the default templates folder you just set. This is where you will need to save it to make it available for your use when creating new workbooks.

Step 4: Give the template a new name if desired.

Step 5: Select **Save.**

To create a new file based on the template, use the following procedure.

Step 1: Select the **File** tab to open the Backstage view.

Step 2: Select **New**

Step 3: Select **Personal**.

Step 4: Select the template you want to use.

Chapter 2 – Sharing Workbooks

This chapter helps you understand the issues concerned with sharing a workbook. First, we will look at how to inspect the workbook for issues. Then, you will learn how to share a workbook and edit a shared workbook. You will also learn about tracking changes to document other users changes and comments. Finally, you will learn how to merge copies of a shared workbook to consolidate the changes.

Inspecting a Document

To inspect a document, use the following procedure.

Step 1: Select the **File** tab from the Ribbon to open the Backstage View.

Step 2: Select **Check for Issues**.

Step 3: Select **Inspect Document**.

Step 4: In the *Document Inspector* dialog box, check the box(es) for the content you want the Inspector to find. Select **Inspect**.

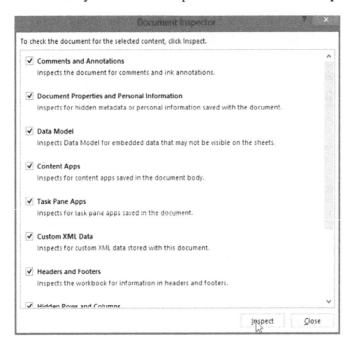

Step 5: The Document Inspector displays the inspection results.

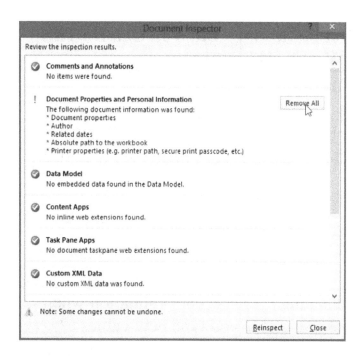

Step 6: Select **Remove All** next to an item if you want to remove it. You can also return to the workbook and make the appropriate changes.

Step 7: Select **Close** when you have finished.

Sharing a Workbook

The following features are not supported in a shared workbook. You can put these items in (and save the workbook) BEFORE you share the workbook. You will not be able to make changes to those features after the workbook is shared.

You Can Not do this is a Shared Workbook	But You Can Do This
Create an Excel table	
Insert or delete blocks of cells	Insert entire rows and columns
Delete worksheets	

You Can Not do this is a Shared Workbook	But You Can Do This
Merge cells or split merged cells	
Sort or filter by formatting	Sort or filter by number, text, or date, apply built-in filters, and filter by using the Search box
Add or change conditional formats	Use existing conditional formats as cell values change
Add or change data validation	Use data validation when you type new values
Create or change charts or PivotChart reports	View existing charts and reports
Insert or change pictures or other objects	View existing pictures and objects
Insert or change hyperlinks	Use existing hyperlinks
Use drawing tools	View existing drawings and graphics
Assign, change, or remove passwords	Use existing passwords
Protect or unprotect worksheets or the workbook	Use existing protection
Create, change, or view scenarios	
Use the Text to Columns	

command	
You Can Not do this is a Shared Workbook	**But You Can Do This**
Group or outline data	Use existing outlines
Insert automatic subtotals	View existing subtotals
Create data tables	View existing data tables
Create or change PivotTable reports	View existing reports
Create or apply slicers	Existing slicers in a workbook are visible after the workbook is shared, but they cannot be changed for standalone slicers or be reapplied to PivotTable data or Cube functions. Any filtering that was applied for the slicer remains intact, whether the slicer is standalone or is used by PivotTable data or Cube functions in the shared workbook.
Create or modify spark lines	Existing spark lines in a workbook are displayed after the workbook is shared, and will change to reflect updated data. However, you cannot create

	new spark lines, change their data source, or modify their properties.
You Can Not do this is a Shared Workbook	**But You Can Do This**
Write, record, change, view, or assign macros	Run existing macros that do not access unavailable features. You can also record shared workbook operations into a macro stored in another nonshared workbook.
Add or change Microsoft Excel 4 dialog sheets	
Change or delete array formulas	Excel will calculate existing array formulas correctly
Work with XML data	
Use a new data form to add new data.	Use a data form to find a record.

To share a workbook, use the following procedure.

Step 1: Select the **Review** tab from the Ribbon.

Step 2: Select **Share Workbook**.

Step 3: In the *Share Workbook* dialog box, check the **Allow changes by more than one user at the same time** box.

Step 4: Select **OK**.

Step 5: In the *Save As* dialog box, enter a new **File Name**, if desired. Navigate to the location where you want to save the workbook and select **Save**.

Note that if there are links in the workbook, you may need to verify them.

Now you can email the people who will share the workbook a link to the file or indicate the location of the file.

Editing a Shared Workbook

To edit a shared workbook, use the following procedure.

Step 1: Open the shared workbook.

Step 2: Make any necessary changes.

Step 3: Save the workbook.

You can see who else has the workbook open on the **Editing** tab of the *Share Workbook* dialog box.

Step 1: Select the **Review** tab from the Ribbon.

Step 2: Select **Share Workbook**.

Select the **Advanced** tab of the *Share Workbook* dialog box to choose to get automatic updates of the other users' changes periodically, with or without saving.

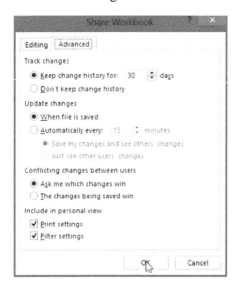

Tracking Changes

To turn on change tracking for a workbook, use the following procedure.

Step 1: Select the **Review** tab from the Ribbon.

Step 2: Select **Share Workbook**.

Step 3: Select the **Advanced** tab of the *Share Workbook* dialog box.

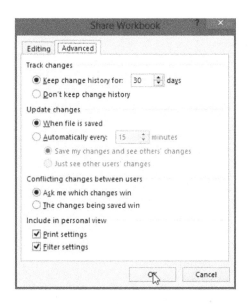

Step 4: Excel keeps the change history for a default of 30 days. You can change the number of days.

Step 5: Select **OK**.

To review the *Highlight Changes* dialog box, use the following procedure.

Step 1: Select the **Review** tab from the Ribbon.

Step 2: Select **Track Changes**. Select **Highlight Changes**.

Step 3: In the *Highlight Changes* dialog box, you can select when to highlight changes, whose changes to highlight and where to highlight the changes. Select **OK** when you have finished making your selections.

Merging Copies of a Shared Workbook

To add the Compare and Merge Workbooks command to the Quick Access toolbar, use the following procedure.

Step 1: Select the arrow next to the Quick Access Toolbar.

Step 2: Select **More Commands** from the menu.

Step 3: In the *Excel Options* dialog box, select **All Commands** from the **Choose Commands From** drop down list.

Step 4: Highlight **Compare and Merge Workbooks** in the left list.

Step 5: Select **Add**.

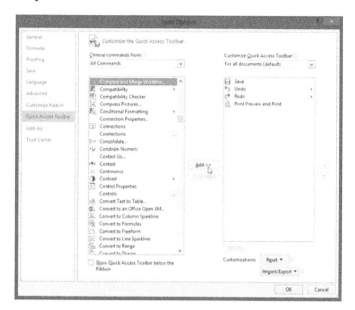

Step 6: Select **OK**.

To compare and merge workbooks, use the following procedure.

Step 1: Open the copy of the shared workbook where you want to merge the changes.

Step 2: On the **Quick Access Toolbar**, click **Compare and Merge Workbooks**.

Step 3: Save the workbook if prompted.

Step 4: In the *Select Files to Merge into Current Workbook* dialog box, select a copy of the workbook that contains the changes that you want to merge. Hold down CTRL or SHIFT to select multiple copies. Select **OK**.

33

Chapter 3 – Performing Advanced Formula and Function Tasks

This chapter will help you with formulas and calculations. We will start with learning how to use the Watch Window, where you can monitor results of different areas of your workbook and even different workbooks related to the one you are changing. Then we will learn about Excel's methodology when calculating worksheets. You will learn how to set the calculation options for the current workbook and for all workbooks. This chapter also explains how to enable or disable automatic workbook calculations. Finally, we will look at the IFERROR function, which can help you evaluate formulas and display specific results if the formula contains an error.

Using the Watch Window

To use the Watch Window, use the following procedure.

Step 1: Select the **Formulas** tab from the Ribbon.

Step 2: Select **Watch Window**.

Step 3: In the *Watch Window*, select **Add Watch**.

Step 4: In the *Add Watch* dialog box, indicate the cells that you want to watch. You can either type the cell references directly into the dialog box, or you can select the cells with your mouse.

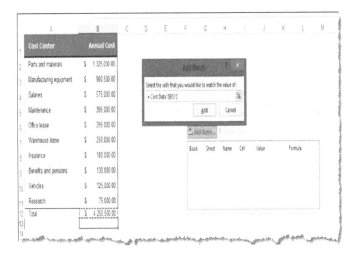

Note that you can select more than one contiguous cell. You can even select cells on another worksheet.

Step 5: Select **Add**.

Step 6: Notice that the Watch Window has started monitoring the selected cells. It indicates the workbook and worksheet where the cell(s) reside, the name of the cell (if you named it), the cell you are monitoring, the current value, and the formula you used to create that value.

Book	Sheet	Name	Cell	Value	Formula
Sample...	Cost ...		B12	$4,250,500.00	=SUM(B2:B11)

Note that you can size the window by selected Size from the arrow in the top right corner. Then drag the corners to the new size.

You can also move the *Watch Window* to a more convenient location on your screen. Just drag the top border to the new location. In this example, it is docked to the top of the screen, just below the Ribbon. You can also dock it to the left or the right side of the screen.

Add more areas to watch and make changes to the watched cells to see the results.

To delete a watch, highlight the item in the *Watch Window* you no longer need and select **Delete Watch**.

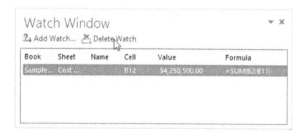

About the Excel Calculation Process

The three stages in the process of calculating data in Excel are:

- Constructing a dependency tree

- Constructing a calculation chain

- Recalculating cells

Dependency Tree and Calculation Chain

Excel uses the dependency tree to determine precedents. Excel uses this dependency tree to construct a calculation chain, which lists all cells that contain formulas in the order in which they should be calculated.

Each time the workbook is recalculated, Excel revises the Calculation chain if it comes across a formula that depends on a cell that has not been calculated. This means that calculation times improve from the first time the worksheet has been opened to the completion of the first few calculation cycles.

Dirty Cells

Anytime you make a structural change to a workbook (including entering a new formula), Excel must reconstruct the dependency tree and calculation train. Excel marks all cells that depend on a new formula or cell of data that you enter as *dirty*. Direct and indirect dependents are marked as dirty. At this time, Excel also detects any circular references and displays a warning message.

Excel re-evaluates the contents of each dirty cell in the order dictated by the calculation chain. With automatic calculations, the recalculation for these cells happens immediately after marking the cells as dirty.

Setting Calculation Options

Use the following procedure to set calculation options at the workbook level.

Step 1: Select the **Formulas** tab from the Ribbon.

Step 2: Select **Calculation Options**.

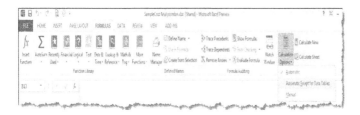

Step 3: Select one of the calculation options.

Step 4: If you do not use **Automatic calculation**, you can use the **Calculate Now** and **Calculate Sheet** commands in the same group on the **Formulas** tab, using the Customize the Ribbon tab on the Excel Options dialog box.

Enabling or Disabling Automatic Workbook Calculations

To use the Options dialog box to set the Calculation Options, use the following procedure.

Note that setting Calculation options in this way applies to the application level rather than the workbook level. That means it applies for all open workbooks.

Step 1: Select the **File** tab from the Ribbon.

Step 2: Select **Options**.

Step 3: Select **Formulas**.

You can also set **Iterative Calculation** in the *Options* dialog box. Check the box and select a number of **Maximum Iterations**. Also indicate the **Maximum change** amount.

Note that the Iterative calculation options are a session-based option. That means that next time you open Excel, you will need to reset the Iterative calculation options.

Using the IFERROR Function to Evaluate Formulas

To use the IFERROR function, use the following procedure.

Step 1: In the cell that includes the formula you want to check, enter =IFERROR. When you start typing, the IFERROR function will display in a drop down menu. You can double-click to select it.

Step 2: Enter an open parenthesis, then the formula that you want to use.

Step 3: Enter a comma after the formula, then the value to display if the formula returns an error. Remember that if you want to use text, it must be in quotation marks.

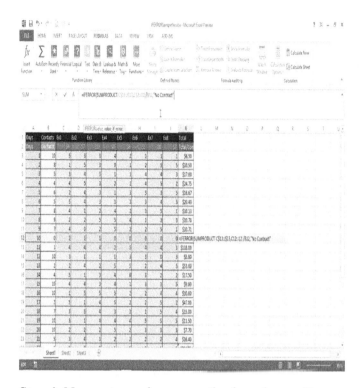

Step 4: Now enter a close parenthesis and press Enter.

Step 5: Notice that when you fill the new formula into all of the cells in Column K, the division by zero errors has been replaced with the words "No Contract."

Chapter 4 – Working with Array Formulas

This chapter introduces using array formulas. We will first look at what array formulas are and some advantages, disadvantages, and rules when using them, as well as an introduction to array constants. Then you will practice creating simple and more advanced arrays.

About Array Formulas

Array formulas allow you to do complex tasks in Excel. For example, you may want to count the number of characters in a range of cells or sum only numbers that meet certain conditions. Array formulas are also known as CSE formulas because of the keystrokes you use to enter the formula (CTRL + SHIFT + ENTER).

An array is a collection of items that, in Excel, can reside in a single row, a single column or multiple rows and columns. A single-row or column array is known as a one-dimensional array (either one-dimensional horizontal or one-dimensional vertical). Multiple row and column arrays are known as two-dimensional arrays. Excel does not allow you to create three-dimensional array formulas.

An array formula can perform multiple calculations on one or more items in the array. You can return either multiple results or a single result.

Array formulas offer several advantages. They provided consistency in your workbook, which helps ensure greater accuracy. They also provide safety from accidentally overwriting a component of the array. Changes to array formulas must be confirmed by pressing CTRL + SHIFT + ENTER. Another advantage is that using array formulas result in smaller file sizes than using several intermediate formulas.

Array formulas also have some disadvantages. Array formulas are typically undocumented in a worksheet, which may cause problems if other users do not understand how to use array formulas. Also, large array formulas can slow down calculations.

Rules for entering and changing multi-cell array formulas

In addition to pressing CTRL+SHIFT+ENTER whenever you need to enter or edit an array formula, multi-cell formulas require some additional rules.

- Select the range of cells to hold your results before you enter the formula.

- You cannot change the contents of an individual cell in an array formula.

- You can move or delete an entire array formula, but you cannot move or delete part of it. In other words, to shrink an array formula, you first delete the existing formula and then start over.

- You cannot insert blank cells into or delete cells from a multi-cell array formula.

Array Constants

You use array constants as a component of array formulas. To create an array constant, you enter a list of items and surround the list with braces. For example, here is a simple array constant: **={1,2,3,4,5}**

A horizontal array is created by separating the constant list items with a comma. You can create a vertical array by using semicolons instead. A two-dimensional array includes definitions for both rows and columns, so the list will use both commas and semicolons.

Constants can include numbers, text, logical values and error values. Numbers can appear in integer, decimal, and scientific formats. Remember to include text in quotation marks (""). Array constants cannot include additional arrays, formulas, or functions.

Creating One-Dimensional and Two-Dimensional Constants

To create a horizontal constant, use the following procedure.

Step 1: In the first row of the blank workbook, enter the following information:

Step 2: Select cells A1 through E1.

Step 3: In the formula bar, enter the following formula

={1,2,3,4,5}

Step 4: Press CTRL + SHIFT + ENTER.

Excel enters the constant into each cell that you selected.

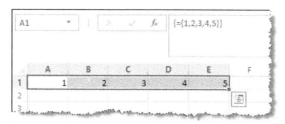

To create a vertical constant, use the following procedure.

Step 1: In the first column of a blank worksheet, enter the following into cells A1 through A5:

1
2
3
4
5

Step 2: Select cells A1 through A5.

Step 3: In the formula bar, enter the following formula

={1;2;3;4;5}

Step 4: Press CTRL + SHIFT + ENTER.

Again, Excel enters the constant into each selected cell.

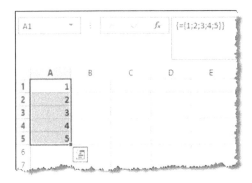

To create a two-dimensional constant, use the following procedure.

Step 1: In a blank worksheet, enter a number from 1 to 12 in each of the first four rows and first four columns, as below:

1	2	3	4
5	6	7	8
9	10	11	12

Step 2: Select cells A1 through D3.

Step 3: In the formula bar, enter the following formula

={1,2,3,4;5,6,7,8;9,10,11,12}

Step 4: Press CTRL + SHIFT + ENTER.

Notice the results.

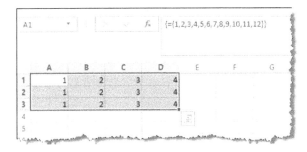

To use an array constant in a formula, use the following procedure.

Step 1: On the sheet from the previous procedures that includes the horizontal constant, copy the following formula in cell A3:

=SUM(A1:E1*{1,2,3,4,5})

Step 2: Press CTRL + SHIFT + ENTER.

Notice that Excel adds brackets around the entire formula. This formula multiplies the values stored in the stored array by the corresponding values in the constant. It is the equivalent of =SUM(A1*1,B1*2,C1*3,D1*4,E1*5).

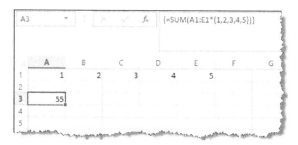

To name an array constant, use the following procedure.

Step 1: Select the **Formulas** tab.

Step 2: Select **Define Name**.

Step 3: In the *New Name* dialog box, enter the name. In this example, we will call it Quarter1.

Step 4: In the Refers to box, enter the following constant. Remember to type the braces manually.

={"January","February","March"}

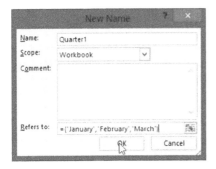

Step 5: Select **OK**.

Now let us try using the named array constant.

Step 1: Select a row of three blank cells in the worksheet.

Step 2: Enter the following formula:

=Quarter1

Step 3: Press CTRL + SHIFT + ENTER.

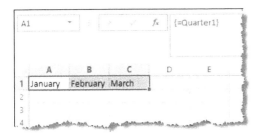

Creating a Simple Array

To create an array from existing values.

Step 1: In the sample workbook, on the Arrays worksheet, select cells C1 through E3.

Step 2: Enter the following formula in the formula bar:

=Data!E1:G3

Step 3: Press CTRL + SHIFT + ENTER.

The following result is displayed.

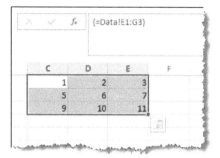

The formula links to the values stored in cells E1 through G3 on the Data worksheet. (You could also accomplish this by putting a separate, unique formula in each cell of the Arrays worksheet).

If you change some of the values on the Data worksheet, those changes appear on the Arrays worksheet. Remember that you will have to follow the Array rules if you need to change any of the data.

To create an array constant from existing values, use the following procedure.

Step 1: In the sample workbook, on the Arrays worksheet, select cells C1 through E3.

Step 2: Press F2 to switch to edit mode.

Step 3: Press F9 to convert the cell references to values.

Excel converts the values into an array constant.

Step 4: Press CTRL+SHIFT+ENTER to enter the array constant as an array formula.

Step 5: Excel replaces the =Data!E1:G3 array formula with the following array constant: ={1,2,3;5,6,7;9,10,11}

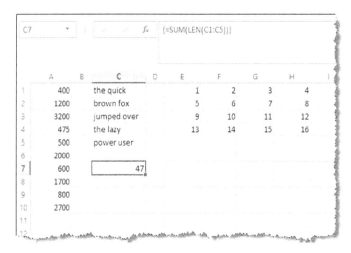

	f_x		{={1,2,3;5,6,7;9,10,11}}	
	C	**D**	**E**	**F**
	1	2	3	
	5	6	7	
	9	10	11	

This means that the link between the Data and Arrays worksheets is no longer there. The Array constant replaces the array formula.

To create an array that counts the characters in a range of cells, use the following procedure.

Step 1: On the Data worksheet, enter the following formula in cell C7:

=SUM(LEN(C1:C5))

Step 2: Press CTRL + SHIFT + ENTER.

The LEN function returns the length of each text string in the range. The SUM function then adds those values together and displays the result in the cell with the formula.

C7				f_x	{=SUM(LEN(C1:C5))}			
	A	**B**	**C**	**D**	**E**	**F**	**G**	**H**
1	400		the quick		1	2	3	4
2	1200		brown fox		5	6	7	8
3	3200		jumped over		9	10	11	12
4	475		the lazy		13	14	15	16
5	500		power user					
6	2000							
7	600		47					
8	1700							
9	800							
10	2700							
11								

To create an array that finds the *N* smallest values in a range, use the following procedure.

Step 1: On the Data worksheet, select cells A12 through A14 to hold the results returned by the array formula.

Step 2: Enter the following formula:

=SMALL(A1:A10,{1;2;3})

Step 3: Press CTRL + SHIFT + ENTER.

The SMALL function is evaluated three times in this formula. The result is the first, second, and third smallest members of the array contained in cells A1:A10. You could add more arguments to the constant to find more values. You could replace the SMALL function with the LARGE function to find the largest values in a range.

A12			f_x	{=SMALL(A1:A10,{1;2;3})}				
	A	B	C	D	E	F	G	H	I
1	400		the quick		1	2	3	4
2	1200		brown fox		5	6	7	8
3	3200		jumped over		9	10	11	12
4	475		the lazy		13	14	15	16
5	500		power user					
6	2000							
7	600		47					
8	1700							
9	800							
10	2700							
11								
12	400							
13	475							
14	500							
15								

You could also use the SUM or AVERAGE functions with this formula, such as

=SUM(SMALL(A1:A10,{1;2;3}))

=AVERAGE(SMALL(A1:A10,{1;2;3;})

To create an array to find the longest text string in a range of cells, use the following procedure.

Step 1: On the Data worksheet, delete the contents of C7.

Step 2: Enter the following formula:

=INDEX(C1:C5,MATCH(MAX(LEN(C1:C5)),LEN(C1:C5),0),1)

Step 3: Press CTRL + SHIFT + ENTER.

Let us examine this formula, starting with the inner elements. The LEN function returns the length of each item, as shown before. The MAX function calculates the largest value among those items. Then the MATCH function calculates the offset, or relative position, of the cell that contains the longest text string. It requires three arguments, which are a lookup value, a lookup array, and a match type. The MATCH type argument is 0 in this case. Finally, the INDEX function has an array and a row and column number within that array as its arguments. The MATCH function provides the cell address.

C7					f_x	{=INDEX(C1:C5,MATCH(MAX{LEN(C1:C5)},LEN(C1:C5),0),1)}				
	A	B	C	D	E	F	G	H	I	J
1	400		the quick		1	2	3	4		
2	1200		brown fox		5	6	7	8		
3	3200		jumped over		9	10	11	12		
4	475		the lazy		13	14	15	16		
5	500		power user							
6	2000									
7	600		jumped over							
8	1700									
9	800									
10	2700									
11										
12	400									
13	475									
14	500									

Creating an Advanced Array

The SUM function in Excel does not work when you try to sum a range that contains an error value, such as #N/A.

To create an array that sums a range that contains error values, use the following procedure.

Step 1: In Cell K35, enter the following formula:

=SUM(IF(ISERROR(K3:K33),"",(K3:K33)))

Step 2: Press CTRL + SHIFT + ENTER.

This formula creates a new array that includes the original values, but does not include the error values.

K35				fx	{=SUM(IF(ISERROR(K3:K33),"",(K3:K33)))}				
	C	D	E	F	G	H	I	J	K	L
25	3	2	4	5	4	3	2	2	$13.14	
26	4	1	4	3	5	2	5	5	$11.00	
27	3	4	5	3	2	0	5	4	$10.67	
28	3	5	3	4	5	2	1	4	$11.22	
29	2	5	4	5	5	3	5	4	$15.38	
30	3	0	5	5	1	4	2	3	$40.00	
31	4	3	5	1	1	1	0	5	$18.50	
32	2	4	2	5	5	2	4	1	$94.00	
33	1	1	4	3	3	5	4	4	$18.60	
34										
35									$672.04	
36										

To create an array that counts the number of error values in a range, use the following procedure.

Step 1: In Cell K37, enter the following formula:

=SUM(IF(ISERROR(K3:K33),1,0))

Step 2: Press CTRL + SHIFT + ENTER.

This formula is similar to the previous one, but instead of omitting the error cells from the sum, it returns the number of error values in the range.

	K37				fx	{=SUM(IF(ISERROR(K3:K33),1,0))}					
	C	D	E	F	G	H	I	J	K	
25	3	2	4	5	4	3	2	2	$13.14	
26	4	1	4	3	5	2	5	5	$11.00	
27	3	4	5	3	2	0	5	4	$10.67	
28	3	5	3	4	5	2	1	4	$11.22	
29	2	5	4	5	5	3	5	4	$15.38	
30	3	0	5	5	1	4	2	3	$40.00	
31	4	3	5	1	1	1	0	5	$18.50	
32	2	4	2	5	5	2	4	1	$94.00	
33	1	1	4	3	3	5	4	4	$18.60	
34										
35									$672.04	
36										
37									2	
38										

In the next example, let us imagine that you need to sum just the positive integers in a range named Sales, which is already defined on Sheet 2.

To create an array that sums values based on conditions, use the following procedure.

Step 1: In cell K 39, enter the following formula:

=SUM(IF(Sales>0,Sales))

Step 2: Press CTRL + SHIFT + ENTER.

The IF function creates an array of positive values and false values. The SUM function ignores the false values.

	C	D	E	F	G	H	I	J	K	L
25	3	2	4	5	4	3	2	2	$13.14	
26	4	1	4	3	5	2	5	5	$11.00	
27	3	4	5	3	2	0	5	4	$10.67	
28	3	5	3	4	5	2	1	4	$11.22	
29	2	5	4	5	5	3	5	4	$15.38	
30	3	0	5	5	1	4	2	3	$40.00	
31	4	3	5	1	1	1	0	5	$18.50	
32	2	4	2	5	5	2	4	1	$94.00	
33	1	1	4	3	3	5	4	4	$18.60	
34										
35									$672.04	
36										
37									2	
38										
39									603.6595	
40										

To create an array that computes an average that excludes zeros, use the following procedure.

Step 1: In cell D35, enter the following formula:

=AVERAGE(IF((D3:D33)<>0,(D3:D33)))

Step 2: Press CTRL + SHIFT + ENTER.

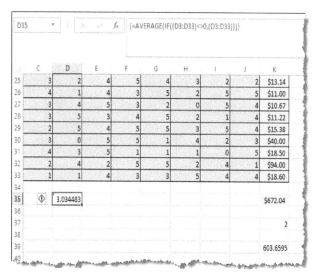

Chapter 5 – Working with Macros

In this chapter, you will learn how to assign a macro you have created to a command button, which you can easily access each time you want to run the macro. You will also learn how to set up a graphical area that causes a macro to run when it is clicked. Similarly, this chapter explains how to run a macro automatically when a spreadsheet is opened. Finally, you will learn how to change a macro.

Assigning a Macro to a Command Button

To assign a new macro to a command key, use the following procedure.

Step 1: Select the **File** tab from the Ribbon to open the Backstage view.

Step 2: Select the **Options** tab on the left.

Step 3: Select **Customize Ribbon**.

Step 4: In the **Choose commands from** drop down list, select Macros.

You will need to create a Custom Group on the Ribbon before you can assign a macro to a Ribbon tab.

Step 1: Select **New Group.**

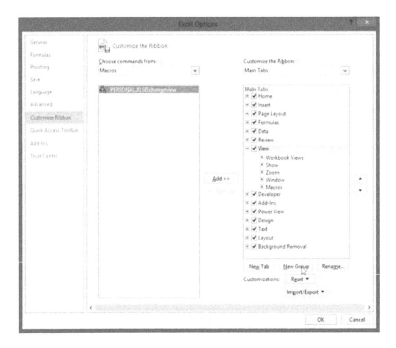

Step 2: Select **Rename**.

Step 3: Enter a new **Display name**.

Step 4: Select **OK**.

Now add the macro to the group.

Step 1: In the Customize the Ribbon list, select the ribbon where you would like to display the Macro command button.

58

Step 2: In the **Choose Command from** list, select your macro.

Step 3: Select **Add**.

Step 4: Select **Rename**.

Step 5: Select an icon for the macro from the list of **Symbols**.

Step 6: Select **OK**.

Now look at the selected Ribbon and see the macro command that you added.

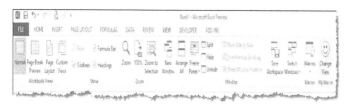

Running a Macro by Clicking an Area of a Graphic Object

To assign a macro to a graphical object, use the following procedure.

Step 1: Insert a shape. To do this, select the **Insert** tab from the Ribbon. Select **Shapes**. Select the shape you want to insert.

Step 2: Right-click on the shape.

Step 3: Select **Assign Macro** from the context menu.

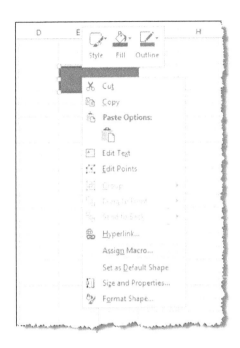

Step 4: Select the **Macro name** from the list. You can choose the location where the **Macro is stored by** selecting a new option from the Macros in drop down list.

Step 5: Select **OK**.

Now try running the macro by clicking on the object.

You can format the shape in any way desired.

Configuring a Macro to Run Automatically Upon Opening the Workbook

To create an Auto_Open macro, use the following procedure.

Step 1: Select the **View** tab from the Ribbon.

Step 2: Select **Macros**.

Step 3: Select **Record Macro.**

Step 4: In the **Macro name** box, enter Auto_Open as the name.

Step 5: In the **Store macro in** list, select the workbook where you want to store the macro from the drop down list.

Step 6: Select **OK**.

Step 7: Perform the actions that you want the macro to perform. For a simple example, simply select **Zoom to Selection** from the **View** tab.

Step 8: Select **Macros** from the **View** tab. Select **Stop Recording**.

Step 9: Save the workbook. You will need to select Excel macro-Enabled Workbook (*.xlsm) from the Save as type drop down list.

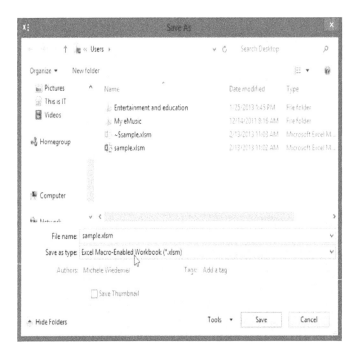

To test out your auto macro, close the workbook and reopen it. The macro is performed as soon as you open the workbook.

Recording an Auto_Open macro has the following limitations:

• If the workbook where you save the Auto_Open macro already contains a VBA procedure in its **Open** event, the VBA procedure for the **Open** event will override all actions in the Auto_Open macro.

• An Auto_Open macro is ignored when a workbook is opened programmatically by using the **Open** method.

• An Auto_Open macro runs before any other workbooks open. Therefore, if you record actions that you want Excel to perform on the default Book1 workbook or on a workbook that is loaded from the XLStart folder, the Auto_Open macro will fail when you restart Excel, because the macro runs before the default and startup workbooks open.

To start a workbook without running an Auto_Open macro, hold down the SHIFT key when you start Excel.

Changing a Macro

To change the name of a macro, use the following procedure.

Step 1: Select the **View** tab from the Ribbon.

Step 2: Select **Macros.**

Step 3: Select **View Macros.**

Step 4: In the *Macro* dialog box, select the name of the macro that you want to change. We will use FillMonths for this example.

Step 5: Select **Edit**.

The Visual Basic Editor opens with your macro. The macro is a sub-routine in the programming. We will make a copy of our FillMonths() macro, or subroutine, and change both of the new macros slightly.

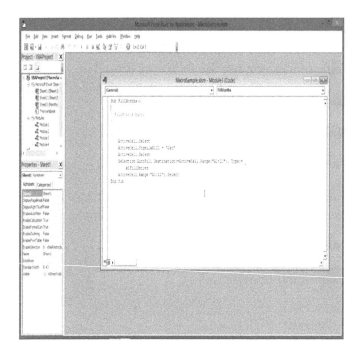

First, we will make a copy of the macro.

Step 1: Select everything from Sub FillMonths() to End Sub.

Step 2: Select Copy. (CTRL + C)

Step 3: Place your cursor below End Sub.

Step 4: Paste by pressing CTRL + V.

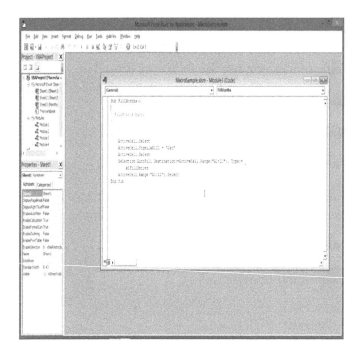

Now we are going to change the name of the first macro.

Step 1: At the top of the first subroutine, enter an R next to FillMonths, to represent, *fill months row*. Remember that macro names cannot contain spaces.

Now we are going to change the name of the second macro. Look for the line that divides the subroutines.

Step 2: Enter a C next to FillMonths, to represent *fill months column*.

Now we are going to change the second macro so that it fills down instead of across and it uses the number representation of the months instead of the names.

Step 3: In the following line, change "Jan " to 1

ActiveCell.FormulaR1C1 = "Jan"

The result should be

ActiveCell.FormulaR1C1 = 1

Step 4: Now change the range so that it is a column. You will need to change **"A1:L1"** to **"A1:A12"** in two places.

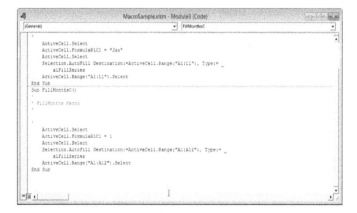

Now when you return to the Macros dialog box, you see that there are two separate macros with the names we assigned. Practice running them to see how they work.

Chapter 6 – Working with Forms

This chapter takes a closer look at forms. Really, all Excel spreadsheets are a type of form where you can enter data. However, we will take a look at data forms and form controls a little more closely as other ways to collect information with more flexibility. You will also learn how to create and use a data form, including adding a new row of data, finding information by navigating or by entering search criteria, and changing or deleting a row of data. Next, we will look at some specific examples of using different types of form controls. This chapter covers the list box control, the combo box control, the spin button control, and the scroll bar control.

About Excel Forms, Form Controls, and Active X Controls

Data Forms

Data forms are a convenient way to display one complete row of information in a range or table without having to scroll horizontally. Data forms work best when you have column headings that can work as your labels and you do not need sophisticated or custom form features.

Excel can automatically generate a built-in data form for a range or table in your worksheet. The form is displayed as a dialog box, in which each label has an adjacent blank text box. There is a maximum of 32 columns you can use for one data form.

Later in the chapter, you will learn how to create a data form, update rows, and delete rows. You will also learn how to navigate using the data form and how to find a row. Data forms can display a formula result as one of the items, but formulas cannot be changed using the data form.

Worksheets with Form and ActiveX Controls

Worksheets already contain some controls as part of the basic functionality of Excel. For example, you can create labels in cells and format them. You can use comments, hyperlinks, background images, data validation and conditional formatting, as well as other features, like controls.

However, you can also add a number of other controls and customize their properties to fine-tune your worksheet. For example, you can use a list box control to make it easier to select from a list of items.

Controls are placed on the drawing canvas of the worksheet, which means that the controls and objects are independent of row and column boundaries. However, you can also set controls to move and resize with a cell.

We will take about form controls and list controls. You can also use objects drawn with Drawing tools as controls, such as AutoShapes, WordArt, SmartArt and text boxes.

Form Controls

Here is a summary of the form controls in Excel 2013:

- Label – identifies the purpose of a cell or text box, or displays descriptive information like titles, captions, pictures or brief instructions

- Group box – groups related controls into one visual unit in a rectangle with a label (optional)

- Button – runs a macro that performs an action

- Check box – turns a value on or off, and is independent of other checkboxes that may appear in the same group

- Option (radio) button – allows a single choice within a set of mutually exclusive choices usually within a group box

- List box – displays a list of one or more items available as a choice and can be controlled as a single-selection list box, a multiple selection list box (must be adjacent choices) or an extended selection list box (allows multiple noncontiguous choices)

- Combo box – combines a text box with a list box to create a drop down list box, which is like a list box, but more compact and requires the user to click the down arrow

- Scroll bar – allows the user to scroll through a range of values either by clicking the arrows or dragging the scroll bar

- Spin button – increases or decreases a value by clicking the up or down arrow

ActiveX Controls

ActiveX controls are much like form controls, except they allow more flexible design requirements, including appearance, behavior, fonts, and other characteristics. Many can be used with or without VBA code, although some can only be used with VBA UserForms. You cannot use ActiveX controls on chart sheets or XLM macro sheets. Here is a summary of the ActiveX controls in Excel 2013:

- Check box – turns a value on or off, and is independent of other checkboxes that may appear in the same group

- Text box – enables you to view type or edit text or data bound to a cell

- Button – runs a macro that performs an action. You cannot assign a macro to run directly from an ActiveX button the same way you can from a form control.

- Option (radio) button – allows a single choice within a set of mutually exclusive choices usually within a group box

- List box – displays a list of one or more items available as a choice and can be controlled as a single-selection list box, a multiple selection list box (must be adjacent choices) or an extended selection list box (allows multiple noncontiguous choices)

- Combo box – combines a text box with a list box to create a drop down list box, which is like a list box, but more compact and requires the user to click the down arrow

- Toggle button – indicates a state (like yes or no or on or off) that alternates between enabled and disabled

- Spin button – increases or decreases a value by clicking the up or down arrow

- Scroll bar – allows the user to scroll through a range of values either by clicking the arrows or dragging the scroll bar

- Label – identifies the purpose of a cell or text box, or displays descriptive information like titles, captions, pictures or brief instructions

- Image – embeds a picture file (such as bitmap, JPEG, or GIF)

- More controls – allows you to choose from additional controls

Using a Data Form

You will need to add the Form button to the Ribbon or the Quick Access Toolbar, use the following procedure to add it to the Quick Access Toolbar.

Step 1: Select the arrow by the Quick Access Toolbar.

Step 2: Select **More Commands**.

Step 3: In the *Excel Options* dialog box, select **All Commands** from the **Choose Commands from** list.

Step 4: Select **Form** from the list on the left.

Step 5: Select **Add**.

Step 6: Select **OK** to close the dialog box.

Now you can create your form, use the following procedure.

Step 7: With your cursor anywhere in the data on the worksheet, select the Form tool from the Quick Access Toolbar.

Your form is automatically created.

To add a new row of data, use the following procedure.

Step 1: In the data form, select **New**.

Step 2: Enter the information into each text field. You can press the TAB key to go to the next field. Press **Enter** to complete the record and go to another new record. Excel extended the worksheet behind the form down for each new record you create.

To find a row by navigating. Use the following controls:

- The scroll bar allows you to move through one row at a time. Select the up or down arrows to move through the data.

- The scroll bar also allows you to move through the data 10 rows at a time. Select the scroll bar in the area in between the arrows.

- **Find Prev** allows you to move to the previous row in the data.

- **Find Next** allows you to move to the next row in the data.

To find a row by searching, use the following procedure.

Step 1: Select **Criteria**.

Excel displays a blank form.

Step 2: Enter information in one or more fields to indicate your criteria. You can select **Clear** to start over. You can also use the following wildcards:

- ? to replace a single character (sm?th finds "smith" and "smyth")

- * to find any number of characters (*east finds "northeast" and "southeast")

- ~ followed by wildcard character finds a question mark, an asterisk or a tilde

Step 2: You can now scroll (**Find Prev** or **Find Next**) through any matching records.

Step 3: Select **Form** to return to the form.

To change the data in a row, use the following procedure.

Step 1: If you have not yet entered the data by pressing **Enter**, you can select **Restore** to return the data to what is stored on the worksheet.

Step 2: Otherwise, first find the row you want to change. Then simply type over the old data.

Step 3: Press **Enter** to update the row.

To delete a row, use the following procedure.

Step 1: Find the row that you want to delete.

Step 2: Select **Delete**.

Step 3: In the confirmation message, select **OK**. Note that you cannot undo a row deletion after you have confirmed it.

Using a List Box Control

To insert a list box form control, use the following procedure.

Step 1: Make sure the **Developer** tab is showing. If not, go to **Options**, **Customize Ribbon** and check the **Developer** checkbox.

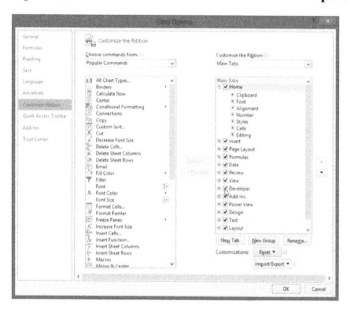

Step 2: Select the **Developer** tab on the Ribbon.

Step 3: Select **Insert**. Select **List Box Form** from the drop down list.

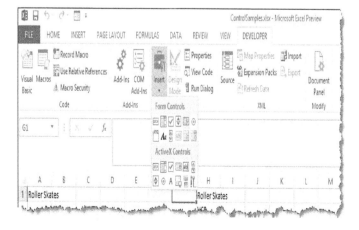

Step 4: Click and drag the mouse to draw the list box. In this example, start at B2 and drag down to E10.

Now we need to format the list box. With the list box still selected, select **Properties** from the **Developer** tab on the Ribbon.

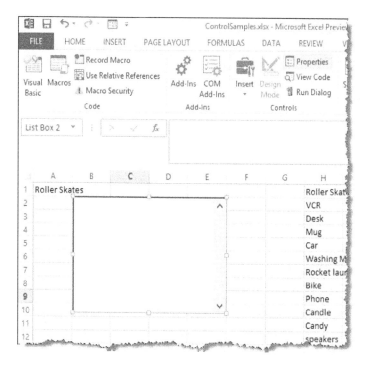

The **Control** tab of the *Format Control* dialog box allows you to indicate an input range and a cell link.

Step 5: In the **Input range** field, enter or select cells H1:H20.

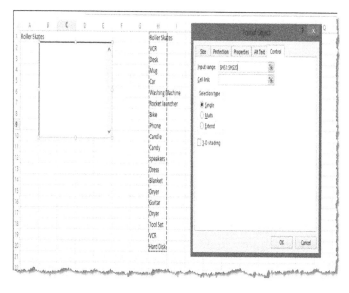

Step 6: The **Cell link** field will put a number value in the linked cell. We will do this so our INDEX formula (which references cell G1) in cell A1 will return the list box choice. Enter or select **G1** for the **Cell link** field.

Step 7: Make sure the **Single** option is selected.

Step 8: Select **OK**.

Step 9: Now click anywhere besides the list box to deselect it. When you select an item in the list, the INDEX formula in cell A1 uses the selection to display the item's name.

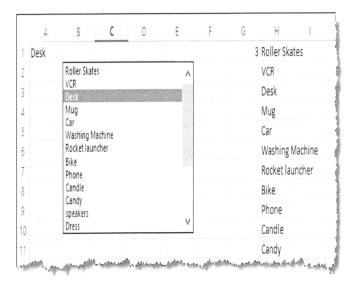

Using a Combo Box Control

To insert a combo box form control, use the following procedure.

Step 1: Select the **Developer** tab.

Step 2: Select **Insert**. Select **Combo Box Form** from the drop down list.

Step 3: Click and drag the mouse to draw the combo box.

Step 4: Right-click the combo box, and select **Format Control** from the drop down list.

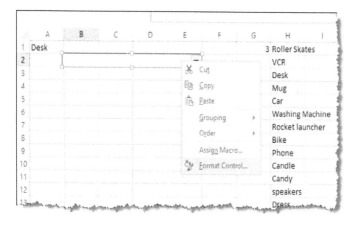

Step 5: In the **Input range** field, enter or select cells H1:H20.

Step 6: The **Cell link** field will put a number value in the linked cell. We will do this so our INDEX formula (which references cell G1) in cell A1 will return the list box choice. Enter or select **G1** for the **Cell link** field.

Step 7: The **Drop down lines** indicates the number of lines that show in the list at one time.

Step 8: Select **OK**.

Step 9: Now click anywhere besides the combo box to deselect it. When you select the arrow and choose an item from the list, the INDEX formula in cell A1 uses the selection to display the item's name.

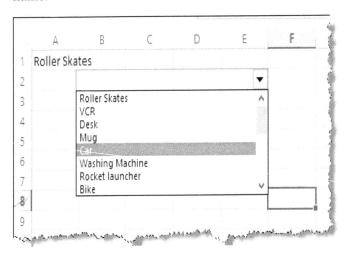

Using a Spin Button Control

To insert a list spin button control, use the following procedure.

Step 1: Select the **Developer** tab.

Step 2: Select **Insert**. Select **Spin Button** from the drop down list.

Step 3: Click and drag the mouse to draw the spin button control.

Step 4: Right-click the spin button control, and select **Format Control** from the drop down list.

Step 5: On the **Control** tab of the *Format Control* dialog box, enter **1** in the **Current Value** field.

Step 6: Also enter **1** as the **Minimum Value** to restrict the top of the spin button to the first item in our list.

Step 7: Enter **20** as the **Maximum value** to specify the maximum number of entries in the list.

Step 8: Enter **1** as the **Incremental Change**.

Step 9: To put a number value in cell G1 for our INDEX formula in this example, enter **G1** in the **Cell link** field.

Step 10: Select **OK**.

Step 11: Now click anywhere besides the spin button to deselect it. When you click the up or down controls, cell G1 is updated. The INDEX formula in cell A1 uses the value in G1 to display the item's name.

Using a Scroll Bar Control

To insert a list scroll bar control, use the following procedure.

Step 1: Select the **Developer** tab.

Step 2: Select **Insert**. Select **Scroll Bar** from the drop down list.

Step 3: Click and drag the mouse to draw the scroll bar control.

Step 4: Right-click the scroll bar control, and select **Format Control** from the drop down list.

Step 5: On the **Control** tab of the *Format Control* dialog box, enter **1** in the **Current Value** field.

Step 6: Also enter **1** as the **Minimum Value** to restrict the top of the scroll bar to the first item in our list.

Step 7: Enter **20** as the **Maximum value** to specify the maximum number of entries in the list.

Step 8: Enter **1** as the **Incremental Change**.

Step 9: In the **Page Change** field, enter **5** to control how much the current value increments if you click inside the scroll bar instead of on the arrows.

Step 10: To put a number value in cell G1 for our INDEX formula in this example, enter **G1** in the **Cell link** field.

Step 11: Select **OK**.

Step 12: Now click anywhere besides the scroll bar to deselect it. When you click the up or down arrows or anywhere in the scroll bar, cell G1 is updated. The INDEX formula in cell A1 uses the value in G1 to display the item's name.

Chapter 7 – Applying Advanced Chart Features

In this chapter, you will learn about some advanced chart features. First, we will look at the different types of trend lines to help you analyze your data. You will also learn how to add a trend line. Then, we will take a look at how to plot one of your data series on a secondary axis. Finally, you will learn how to save a chart you have formatted to your liking as a chart template to be available for use when creating other new charts.

About Trend Lines

You can add one of six different trend or regression types, depending on the type of data that you have.

Note that a trend line is most accurate when its R-squared value is at or near 1. You can display the R-squared value that Excel calculates on your chart.

The following types of trend lines are available.

Linear trend line – this trend line is a best-fit straight line used with simple linear sets.

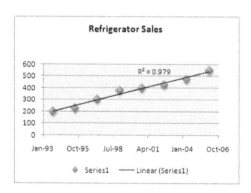

Logarithmic trend line – this trend line is a best-fit curved line used when the rate of change in the data increases or decreases quickly and then levels out. It can use either negative or positive values.

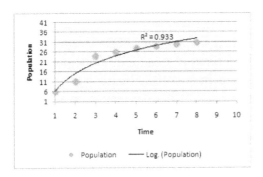

Polynomial trend line – this trend line is a curved line that is used when data fluctuates, such as to analyze gains and losses over a large data set. The polynomial order can be determined by the number of fluctuations in the data or by how many hills and valleys appear in the curve. For example, an Order 2 polynomial trend line has one hill or valley; order 3 has 2 hills or valley, and so on.

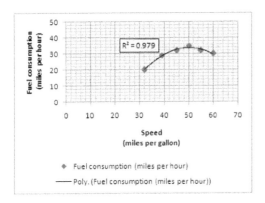

Power trend line – this trend line is a curved line that is used with data sets that compare measurements that increase at a specific rate. Data sets for this type of trend line cannot include 0 or negative values.

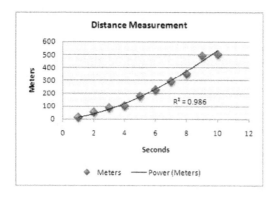

Exponential trend line – this trend line is a curved line that is used with data sets that rise or fall at a constantly increasing rate. Data sets for this type of trend line cannot include 0 or negative values.

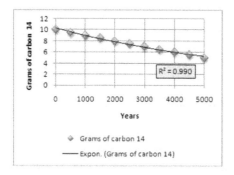

Moving Average Trend Lines – this trend line smooths fluctuations in data to show a pattern or trend more clearly. It uses a specific number of data points in an average to display the points in the line, such as 2 periods to create the first point in the trend line.

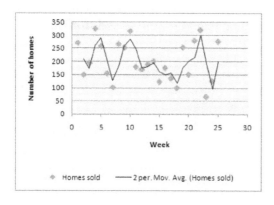

Add a Trend Line

To add a Trend Line to a chart, use the following procedure.

Step 1: Select the chart in your worksheet.

Step 2: Select the data series that you want to plot. A colored border appears around that area in the data.

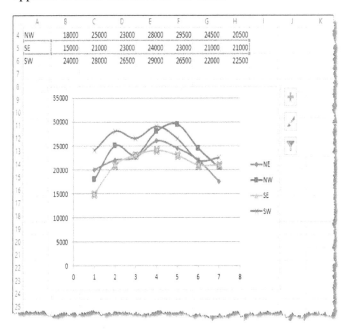

Step 3: Select the plus sign icon from the right side of the chart.

Step 4: Select the small arrow to the right of **Trendlines**.

Step 5: Select the type of trendline that you want to add from the list.

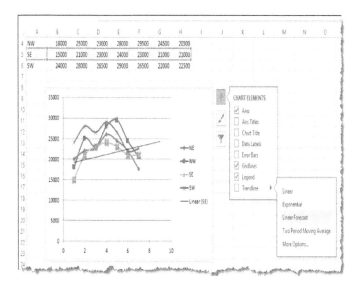

Step 6: If you did not select the specific data series and the chart has more than one, Excel displays a dialog box to help you choose the correct series.

Excel adds the Trendline.

Note that if you select **More Options** from the Trendline choices, Excel will open the Format Trendline pane, where you have several additional options for formatting your trendline.

Using Secondary Axes

To add a secondary vertical axis, use the following procedure.

Step 1: Select the chart.

Step 2: Select the **Chart Tools Format** tab.

Step 3: Select the Chart Elements box arrow and select the data series that you want to plot along a secondary vertical axis.

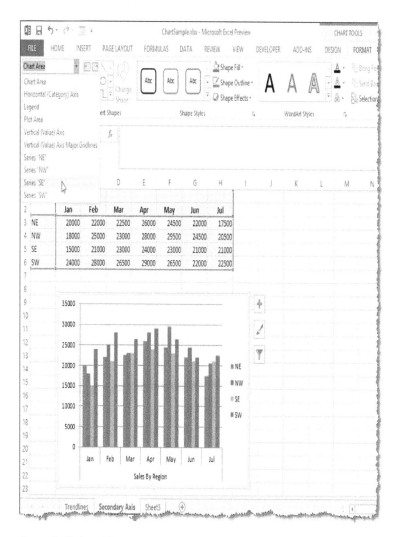

Step 4: Select **Format Selection** from the **Chart Tools Format** tab on the Ribbon.

Step 5: Excel displays the *Format Data Series* pane. In the *Format Data Series* pane, select **Secondary Axis** under **Plot Series On**. The *Format Data Series* pane stays open so that you can format other aspects of the selected data series if desired.

In the following illustration, the chart type for the secondary axis has also been changed. With the secondary axis still selected, just go to the **Chart Tools Design** tab and select **Change Chart Type**.

In the *Change Chart Type* dialog box, your chart is automatically shown as a Custom Combination chart. You can use the drop down lists next to each data series to select another chart option for that data series.

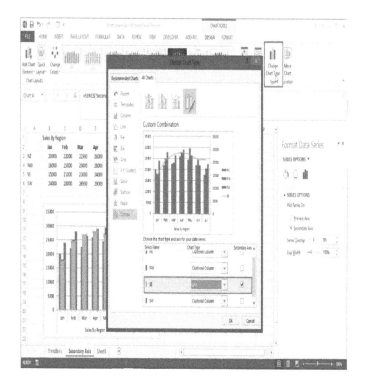

Using Chart Templates

To save a chart as a template, use the following procedure.

Step 1: Right-click the chart.

Step 2: Select **Save As Template**.

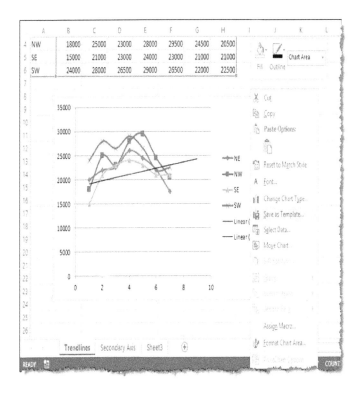

Step 3: In the *Save Chart Template* dialog box, enter a **File name** for the template.

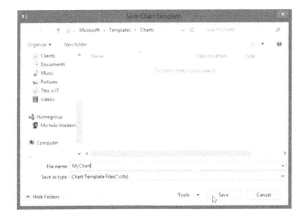

Step 4: Leave the file location as is, if you want the chart template to be available on the **Insert** tab when you select **Charts** or when you select **Change Chart Type**.

Step 5: Select **Save**.

To insert a chart based on their templates, use the following procedure.

Step 1: Select the data you want to use for your chart. You may want to copy the data from the Secondary Axis or Trendlines sheet in the sample file to Sheet 3 for this example.

Step 2: Select the **Insert** tab from the Ribbon.

Step 3: Select **Recommended Charts**.

Step 4: Select the **All Charts** tab.

Step 5: Select the **Templates** option from the left.

Step 6: Select the template that you have previously saved.

Step 7: Select **OK** to insert the chart.

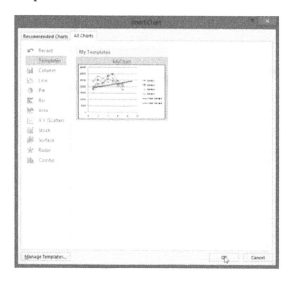

Chapter 8 – Working with Slicers and Timelines

This chapter explains slicers and timelines. You will learn how to create a slicer in an existing table. You will also learn how to format a slicer. Finally, we will discuss how to disconnect or delete a slicer.

About Slicers and Timelines

Slicers were added in Excel2010 to filter PivotTable data. In Excel 2013, you can now use slicers to filter any table data. Slicers clearly indicate what data is shown in the table after you filter the data. They include buttons so that you can quickly filter data without having to use drop down lists to find the items you want to filter. Timelines are a type of slicer that is specific to date ranges.

A slicer typically displays the following elements:

- The slicer header – indicates the category of the items in the slicer.

- Unselected filtering button – indicates that the item is not included in the filter.

- Selected filtering button – indicates that the item is included in the filter.

- **Clear Filter** button – removes the filter by selecting all items in the slicer.

- A scroll bar – enables scrolling when there are more items than are currently visible in the slicer.

- Border moving and resizing controls – allow you to change the size and location of the slicer.

Using slicers

To filter your data, just select one or more of the buttons in the slicer.

You will likely that you will create more than once slicer to filter a data table or PivotTable report.

You can create a slicer that is associated with the current data table or PivotTable. You can also create a copy of a slicer.

Once you create a slicer, it appears on the worksheet alongside the table data, in a layered display if you have more than one. You can move or resize it as needed. Once created, a slicer can also be used with another table or PivotTable.

You can create slicers that work with the current data table or PivotTable or you can create a stand-alone slicer that can be associated with any other table at a later time. Stand-alone slicers can be referenced by Online Analytical Processing (OLAP) Cube functions.

Creating a Slicer in an Existing Table

To create a slicer in an existing table, use the following procedure.

Step 1: Place your cursor anywhere in the table.

Step 2: Select the **Insert** tab from the Ribbon.

Step 3: Select **Slicer**.

Step 4: In the *Insert Slicers* dialog box, select the check box(es) of the fields from the table for which you want to create a slicer.

Step 5: Select **OK**.

Step 6: To apply your filters, just select the buttons for the items you want to include. You can hold down the CTRL key while selecting to choose more than one button.

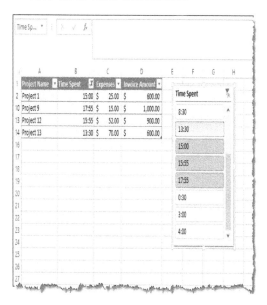

Formatting a Slicer

Note that when you select the slicer object, the **Slicer Tools Options** tab displays on the Ribbon, giving you additional tools to adjust your slicer settings, apply a new slicer style, or arrange and size the slicer object or the buttons.

To format a slicer, use the following procedure.

Step 1: Select the slicer that you want to format.

Step 2: Select the **Slicer Tools Options** tab from the Ribbon.

Step 3: You can select a new Style from the **Slicer Styles** area.

Step 4: Or, you can select the arrows next to **Slicer Styles** and select **New Slicer Style**.

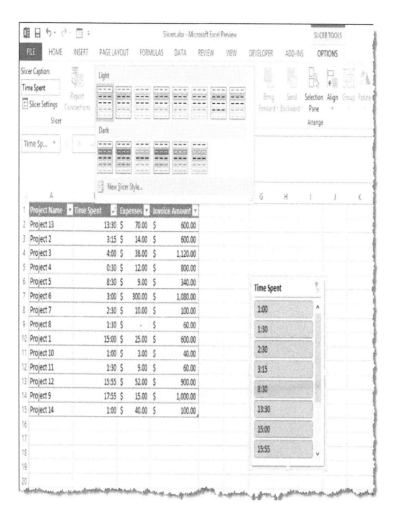

Step 5: In the *New Slicer Style* dialog box, enter a **Name** for the new style.

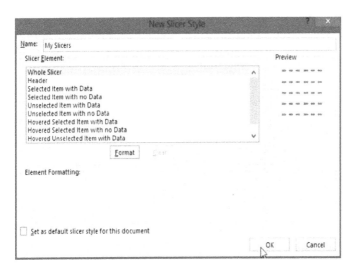

Step 6: Select the **Slicer Element** that you want to format from the list.

Step 7: Select **Format**. You can change the Font, Border, and Fill colors for each element.

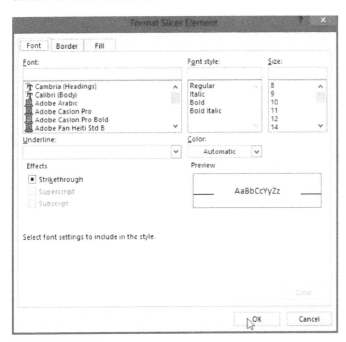

Step 8: Select **OK** when you have finished formatting the selected element.

Step 9: Select **OK** when you have finished formatting all of the desired elements. You can check the **Set as default slicer quick style for this document** check box if desired.

Practice adjusting the size for the slicer and buttons as well.

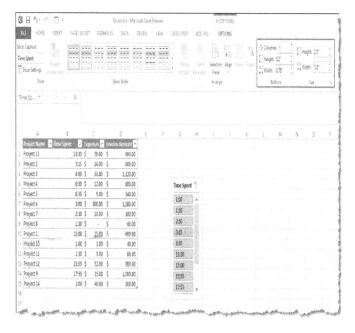

Using a Timeline

To create a timeline in an existing table, use the following procedure.

Step 1: Place your cursor anywhere in the table.

Step 2: Select the **Insert** tab from the Ribbon.

Step 3: Select **Timeline**.

Step 4: In the *Insert Timelines* dialog box, select the check box(es) of the fields from the table for which you want to create a timeline.

Step 5: Select **OK**.

Step 6: Click a period on the timeline to include the date range you want to include in the PivotTable. You can also drag the edges of the timeline to expand the date range shown in the PivotTable. Remember that the timeline is interactive, so feel free to experiment.

Step 7: You can change the period available in the slicer by clicking on the arrow next to the period shown (in this example, Months). Select a new period from the drop down list.

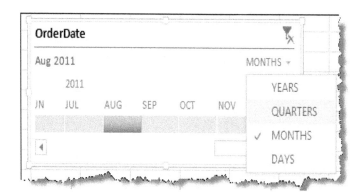

Review the Timeline Tools Options tab on the Ribbon and the Format Timeline pane. You can open the Format Timeline pane using the small square next to the Size group on the Timeline Tools Options tab on the Ribbon.

Chapter 9 – Working with Multiple Tables, Relationships, and External Data

The Data Model in Excel 2013 is a new approach for integrating data from multiple tables. It actually builds a relational data source inside an Excel workbook, but it is virtually transparent. Data models provide the tabular data that is used in PivotTables, PivotCharts, and Power View reports. In this chapter, you will learn how to connect to a new external data source and create a PivotTable using an external data connection. You will use PivotTables to analyze data in multiple tables. You will also learn how to create relationships between tables.

Connecting to a New External Data Source

To connect to an external data source from an Access Database, use the following procedure.

Step 1: Select the **Data** tab from the Ribbon.

Step 2: Select **From Access.**

Step 3: In the *Select Data Source* dialog box, navigate to the location of the database you want to use and select **Open**.

Step 4: In the *Select Table* dialog box, check the box for the table to which you want to connect. If you would like to select more than one table or query, check the **Enable Selection of multiple tables** box. You will use multiple tables later in this chapter, so include more than one table.

Step 5: Select **OK**.

Step 6: In the *Import Data* dialog box, you can chose to create a connection only or a Table, PivotTable Report, PivotChart, or Power View Report. In this example, we will just create the connection.

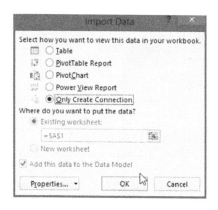

Creating a PivotTable Using an External Data Connection

To create a PivotTable using an existing external data connection, use the following procedure.

Step 1: Select the **Insert** tab from the Ribbon.

Step 2: Select **PivotTable**.

Step 3: In the *Create PivotTable* dialog box, select **Use an external data source**.

Step 4: Select **Choose Connection**.

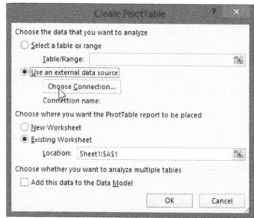

Step 5: In the *Existing Connections* dialog box, select the Connection that you want to use. You can use the **Show** drop down list to narrow the list of connections available.

Step 6: Select **Open**.

Step 7: In the *Create PivotTable* dialog box, choose where to place the new PivotTable.

Step 8: Select **OK**.

Excel adds an empty PivotTable and shows the Field pane so that you create the PivotTable you need.

Working with PivotTables Based on Multiple Tables

A relationship matches data in two tables to create an association. Relationships allow you to use fields from multiple tables, even when the tables originate from different sources. Each table should have a meaningful name to help you identify them when creating the relationship.

One column in one of the tables should have unique, non-duplicate data values.

To work with the PivotTable Fields pane when the PivotTable is based on multiple tables (or a data connection with multiple tables).

Step 1: The Field pane contains all of the tables you selected when you imported the data. You can expand or compress the fields for each table by clicking on the plus or minus signs.

Step 2: Add the fields to the PivotTable report as you would for any PivotTable. You can add fields from any table to the VALUES, ROWS, or COLUMNS area.

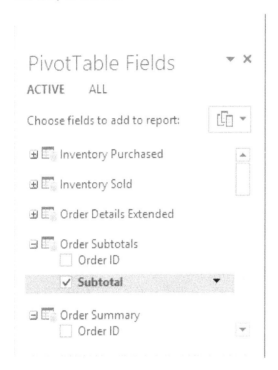

Step 3: If you select fields from tables that are not already related, Excel displays the warning: Relationships between tables may be needed. Select **Create**.

110

Step 4: In the *Create Relationship* dialog box, select the first **Table** from the drop down list. In a one-to-many relationship, this table should be on the many side.

Step 5: Select the **Column** from that table to use in the relationship. This column should have unique values that match the values in the Related Column.

Step 6: Select the **Related Table** from the drop down list. This table should have at least one column of data that is related to the table you just selected.

Step 7: Select the **Column** from that table to use in the relationship from the drop down list.

Step 8: Select **OK**.

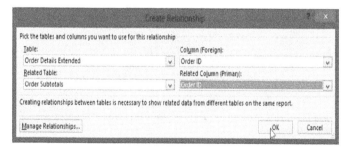

Chapter 10 – Working with Power View

Power View is an interactive way to explore, visualize, and present data that encourages ad-hoc reporting. This chapter will introduce you to Power View with lessons that include downloaded data from the Windows Azure Marketplace to learn how to create a Power View sheet, add additional tables to the data model used by the Power View Sheet and add an additional chart and change it to a map.

About Power View

Make sure that the PowerPivot Add-in is enabled, use the following procedure.

Step 1: Select the **File** tab to open the Backstage View.

Step 2: Select **Options**.

Step 3: Select **Add-ins**.

Step 4: From the **Manage** drop down list, select COM Add-ins.

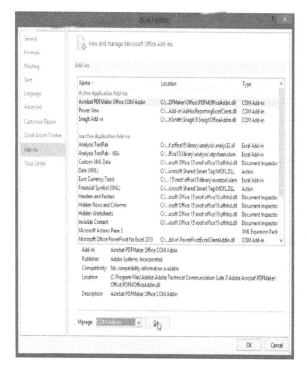

Step 5: Check the **Enable PowerPivot** box.

Step 6: Select **OK**.

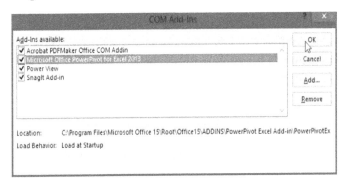

Creating a Power View Sheet

To download the sample data, which creates a data model, use the following procedure.

Step 1: Select the **Power Pivot** tab from the Ribbon. You may need to restart Excel after enabling the Add-in.

Step 2: Select **Manage Data Model**.

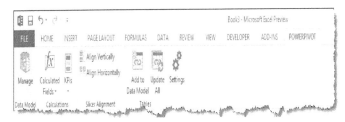

Step 3: In the *PowerPivot for Excel* window, select **Get External Data**. Select **From Data Service**. Select **From Windows Azure Marketplace**.

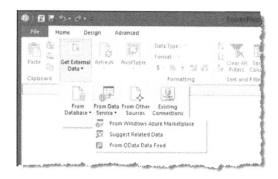

Step 4: In the *Table Import Wizard* window, you can filter the list of options. To find the one for this lesson, select the following filters: **Free** and **Transportation and Navigation**.

Step 5: Next to **US Air Carrier Flight Delays**, select **Subscribe**.

Step 6: Sign in with your Microsoft account. If necessary, create a Windows Azure Marketplace account. Continue making selections until you have finished subscribing to the information.

Step 7: At the end of the sample data, choose **Select Query**.

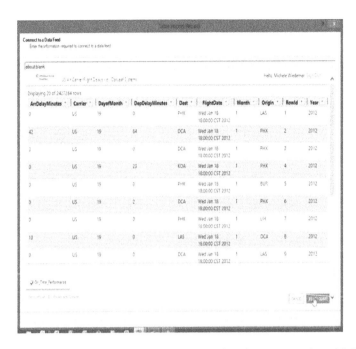

Step 8: You can change the name for the connection, if desired. Select **Next**.

Step 9: Select **Preview & Filter** from the *Table Import Wizard*.

Step 10: Select **OK** to import all of the data. Select **Finish**. Be aware that this may take some time.

To create a Power View sheet, use the following procedure.

Step 1: Select the **Insert** tab from the Ribbon.

Step 2: Select **Power View Reports**.

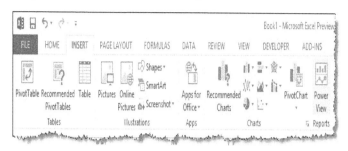

Now let us add some fields to the report.

Step 1: Expand the On_Time_Performance table.

Step 2: Check the **Carrier** box and the **ArrDelayMintues** box.

Step 3: In the **Values** box, select the arrow next to ArrDelayMinutes and select **Sum**. Now you have aggregates per carrier.

Now we will select a chart type.

Step 1: Select the **Design** tab from the Ribbon.

Step 2: Select **Column Chart**. Select **Clustered**.

Step 3: Let us add another field. In the **Field** list, drag DepDelayMinutes to the Values box under ArrDelayMinutes.

Notice that some carriers are better at on-time arrivals, while some are better at on-time departures.

Add a Table to the Data Model

To add a table to the data model, use the following procedure.

Step 1: Go to this site: http://www.airfarewatchdog.com/pages/3799702/airline-letter-codes/.

Step 2: Copy the two columns including the codes and the airline carrier names.

Step 3: On a blank worksheet in your workbook, enter the following headings in cell A1 and B1, respectively: AirlineCode and AirlineName

Step 4: In cell A2, paste the data you copied from the website.

Step 5: Format the data as a table.

Step 6: On the **Table Tools Design** tab, rename the table Airlines.

Step 7: Also rename the worksheet Airlines.

Now we will relate the tables in Power View, use the following procedure.

Step 1: Return to the Power View sheet.

Step 2: Your Airlines table should be in the Field list. If not, select **All** from the Field list.

Step 3: Select the column chart.

Step 4: Remove Carrier from the Axis box.

Step 5: Expand the Airlines tab to check the AirlineName box.

Excel displays the "Relationships between tables may be needed" message.

Step 6: Select **Create**.

Step 7: Select **Airlines** as the first table.

Step 8: Select **AirlineCode** as the column.

Step 9: Select **On_Time_Performance** as the second table.

Step 10: Select **Carrier** as the column.

Step 11: The message warning about the relationship just means that a primary key is created instead of a foreign key.

Step 12: Select **OK**.

To get the airport code data added to the data model, use the following procedure.

Step 1: Go to this site: http://www.airportcodes.us/us-airports.htm.

Step 2: Copy the four columns, including the code, name, city and state without the table heading.

Step 3: Add a new sheet to your workbook.

Step 4: Paste the data in cell A1.

Step 5: Rename the columns so that we can relate the data.

- Code = AirportCode

- Name = AirportName

- City = AirportCity

- State = AirportState

Step 6: Format the data as a table.

Step 7: On the **Table Tools Design** tab, rename the table **Airports**.

Step 8: Also rename the worksheet Airports.

Step 9: Return to the Power View sheet.

Step 10: Remove **Origin** from the Axis box.

Step 11: Expand the Airports table and check the **AirportName** box.

Step 12: Select **Create** in the message to create the appropriate relationships.

Step 13: Select **Airports** as the first table.

Step 14: Select **AirportCode** as the column.

Step 15: Select **On_Time_Performance** as the related table.

Step 16: Select **Origin** as the column.

Step 17: Select **OK**.

Adding a Map to a Power View Report

To create another chart, use the following procedure.

Step 1: You can start another visualization not related to your current fields by clicking on the blank area outside the previous chart.

Step 2: In the **Field** list, on the **On_Time_Performance** table, check the **Origin** box. Also check the **DepDelayMinutes** box.

Step 3: Select the arrow next to DepDelayMinutes and select **Average**.

Step 4: Let us decrease the decimal for that column. Click on the column and use the Decrease Decimal tool on the Design tab of the Ribbon.

Step 5: Now let us convert this table to a bar chart. Select **Bar Chart** from the **Design** tab on the Ribbon. Select **Stacked Bar**.

Step 6: You can move and resize the chart to maximize what you can see with the available real estate on the sheet.

To create a map, use the following procedure.

Step 1: Select the Airports chart.

Step 2: Select the **Design** tab from the Ribbon.

Step 3: Select **Map**.

Step 4: If Power View puts AirportName in the Color box, drag it to the Locations box.

Step 5: Select the plus sign in the upper right corner of the map to zoom in. Use the cursor to reposition the map.

To filter the map, use the following procedure.

Step 1: Select the map.

Step 2: In the **Filters** area, select Map.

Step 3: Select Average of DepDelayMinutes.

Step 4: Drag the left side of the scroll bar to show only delays that are greater than 10 minutes.

Additional Titles

The Technical Skill Builder series of books covers a variety of technical application skills. For the availability of titles please see https://www.silvercitypublications.com/shop/. Note the Master Class volume contains the Essentials, Advanced, and Expert (when available) editions.

Current Titles

Microsoft Excel 2013 Essentials

Microsoft Excel 2013 Advanced

Microsoft Excel 2013 Expert

Microsoft Excel 2013 Master Class

Microsoft Word 2013 Essentials

Microsoft Word 2013 Advanced

Microsoft Word 2013 Expert

Microsoft Word 2013 Master Class

Microsoft Project 2010 Essentials

Microsoft Project 2010 Advanced

Microsoft Project 2010 Expert

Microsoft Project 2010 Master Class

Microsoft Visio 2010 Essentials

Microsoft Visio 2010 Advanced

Microsoft Visio 2010 Master Class

Coming Soon

Microsoft Access 2013 Essentials

Microsoft Access 2013 Advanced

Microsoft Access 2013 Expert

Microsoft Access 2013 Master Class

Microsoft PowerPoint 2013 Essentials

Microsoft PowerPoint 2013 Advanced

Microsoft PowerPoint 2013 Expert

Microsoft PowerPoint 2013 Master Class

Microsoft Outlook 2013 Essentials

Microsoft Outlook 2013 Advanced

Microsoft Outlook 2013 Expert

Microsoft Outlook 2013 Master Class

Microsoft Publisher 2013 Essentials

Microsoft Publisher 2013 Advanced

Microsoft Publisher 2013 Master Class

Windows 7 Essentials

Windows 8 Essentials

www.ingramcontent.com/pod-product-compliance
Lightning Source LLC
Chambersburg PA
CBHW071549080326
40690CB00056B/1575